D0649468

the gift of love

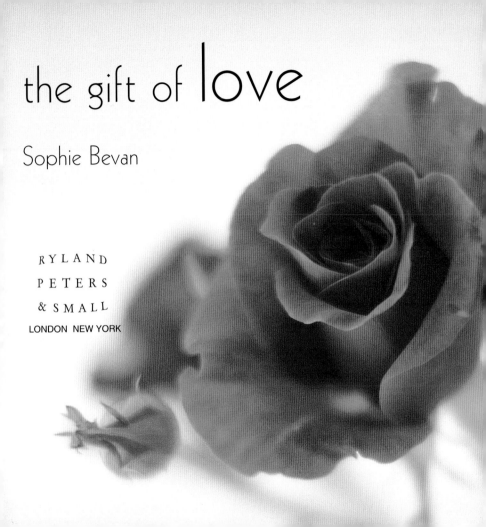

the gift of love

Sophie Bevan

RYLAND
PETERS
& SMALL
LONDON NEW YORK

Designer **Luana Gobbo**

Senior Editor **Clare Double**

Picture Research **Claire Hector,**

Emily Westlake

Production **Deborah Wehner**

Art Director **Gabriella Le Grazie**

Publishing Director **Alison Starling**

Editorial Consultant **Christina Rodenbeck**

First published in the
United States in 2004
by Ryland Peters & Small, Inc.
519 Broadway, 5th Floor
New York NY 10012
www.rylandpeters.com

10 9 8 7 6 5 4 3 2

Text, design, and photographs
© Ryland Peters & Small 2004

ISBN 1 84172 622 2

Printed and bound in China

contents

06 romance

26 desire

46 commitment

64 credits

romance

Those who have courage to love should have courage to suffer.

ANTHONY TROLLOPE (1815–1882),
FROM *THE BERTRAMS*

Though I would
conceal,
In my face it yet appears,
My fond, secret love:
So much that he asks of me,
"Does not something
trouble you?"

TAIRA NO KANEMORI (10TH CENTURY)

How do I love thee?

Let me count the ways.
I love thee to the depth
   and breadth and height
My soul can reach, when
   feeling out of sight
For the ends of Being and
   ideal Grace.

ELIZABETH BARRETT BROWNING (1806–1861),
SONNETS FROM THE PORTUGUESE 43

Love is life. All, everything that I
understand, I understand only because
I love. Everything is, everything exists,
only because I love. Everything is united
by it alone.

LEO TOLSTOY (1828–1910), FROM *WAR AND PEACE*

One word frees us of all the weight and pain in life. That word is love.

SOPHOCLES (C.495–C.406 BC)

Love conquers all: let us, too, yield to love.

VIRGIL (70–19 BC), *ECLOGUES*

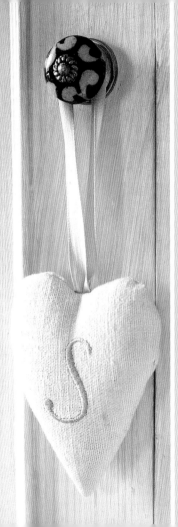

Take my heart; I shall
have it all the more;
Plucking the flowers, we
keep the plant in bloom.

EDMOND ROSTAND (1868–1918),
CYRANO DE BERGERAC

The lunatic, the
lover, and the poet,
Are of imagination
all compact.

WILLIAM SHAKESPEARE (1564–1616),
A MIDSUMMER NIGHT'S DREAM

Who travels for love
finds a thousand miles not
longer than one.

JAPANESE PROVERB

One kind kiss before
    we part,
Drop a tear and bid adieu;
Though we sever, my fond heart
Till we meet shall pant for you.

ROBERT DODSLEY (1703–1764),
THE PARTING KISS

Here with a Loaf of Bread beneath the Bough,
A Flask of Wine, a Book of Verse—and Thou
Beside me singing in the Wilderness—
And Wilderness is Paradise enow.

OMAR KHÁYYAM (C.1050–C.1123),
THE RUBAIYAT OF OMAR KHÁYYAM

Love means the pre-cognitive flow ... it is the honest state before the apple.

D. H. LAWRENCE (1885–1930)

When those red berries come
   in springtime,
Flushing on your southland branches,
Take home an armful, for my sake,
As a symbol of our love.

WANG WEI (699–761), *ONE-HEARTED*

My bounty is as boundless
as the sea,
My love as deep; the more
I give to thee,
The more I have, for both
are infinite.

WILLIAM SHAKESPEARE (1564–1616),
ROMEO AND JULIET

desire

Licence my roving
hands, and let them go,
Before, behind, between,
above, below.

JOHN DONNE (1573–1631),
TO HIS MISTRESS GOING TO BED

. . . once he drew
with one long kiss my whole
soul through my lips . . .

ALFRED, LORD TENNYSON (1809–1892), *FATIMA*

Consumed by fire with my
love for you.
I remember what you said to me.
I am thinking of your love for me.
I am torn by your love for me.

KWAKIUTL POEM (c.1896)

Let him kiss me with the kisses of his
mouth: for thy love is better than wine.

THE BIBLE, SONG OF SOLOMON 1:2

God is Love—I dare say. But what a mischievous devil Love is!

SAMUEL BUTLER (1835–1902), *NOTEBOOKS*

Let us roll all our strength and all
Our sweetness up into one ball,
And tear our pleasures with rough strife
Thorough the iron gates of life:
Thus, though we cannot make our sun
Stand still, yet we will make him run.

ANDREW MARVELL (1621–1678), *To His Coy Mistress*

Let us together closely
lie and kiss,
There is no labor, nor
no shame in this;
This hath pleased, doth
please, and long will
please; never
Can this decay, but is
beginning ever.

PETRONIUS ARBITER (1ST CENTURY AD),
TRANSLATED BY BEN JONSON

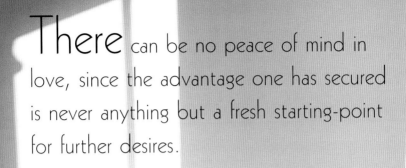

There can be no peace of mind in love, since the advantage one has secured is never anything but a fresh starting-point for further desires.

MARCEL PROUST (1871–1922), *REMEMBRANCE OF THINGS PAST*

. . . **yet** he turn'd once more to look
At the sweet sleeper,—all his soul was shook,—
She press'd his hand in slumber; so once more
He could not help but kiss her and adore.

JOHN KEATS (1795–1821), *ENDYMION*

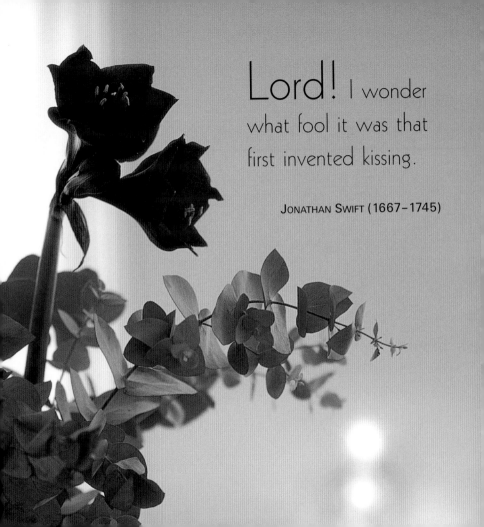

Lord! I wonder what fool it was that first invented kissing.

JONATHAN SWIFT (1667–1745)

What arms and shoulders did I touch and see

How apt her breasts were to be pressed
    by me,
How smooth a belly under her waist saw I,
How large a leg, and what a lusty thigh.
To leave the rest, all liked me passing well;
I clinged her naked body, down she fell:
Judge you the rest, being tired she bade
    me kiss;
Jove send me more such afternoons as this!

OVID (43 BC–17 AD), *ELEGY TO HIS MISTRESS*
TRANSLATED BY CHRISTOPHER MARLOWE

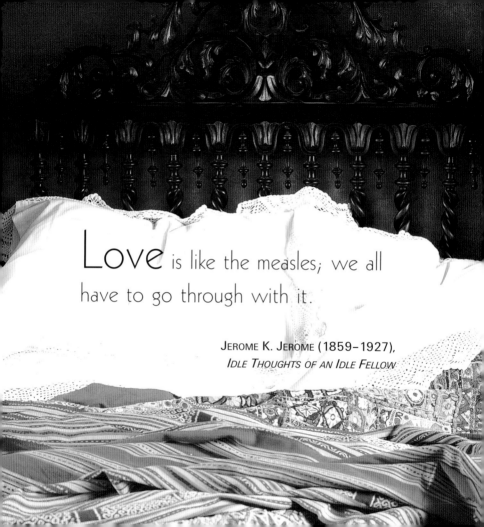

Love is like the measles; we all have to go through with it.

JEROME K. JEROME (1859–1927),
IDLE THOUGHTS OF AN IDLE FELLOW

I am he that aches with amorous love;
Does the earth gravitate? Does not all
   matter, aching, attract all matter?
So the body of me to all I meet or know.

WALT WHITMAN (1819–1892), *I AM HE THAT ACHES WITH LOVE*

The moment we indulge our affections, the earth is metamorphosed; there is no winter and no night; all tragedies, all ennuis, vanish, —all duties even.

RALPH WALDO EMERSON (1803–1882), *ESSAYS*

Ah! when will this long weary day have end,
And lend me leave to come unto my love?

EDMUND SPENSER (1552–1599),
EPITHALAMION

. . . the utmost share
Of my desire shall be
Only to kiss that air
That lately kissed thee.

ROBERT HERRICK (1591–1674),
TO ELECTRA

Clouds bring back
to mind her dress, the
flowers her face.
Winds of spring caress the
rail where sparkling dew-
drops cluster.
If you cannot see her by the
jeweled mountain top,
Maybe on the moonlit Jasper
Terrace you will meet her.

LI BAI (701–762), *A SONG OF PURE HAPPINESS I*

commitment

Same old slippers,
Same old rice,
Same old glimpse of
Paradise.

WILLIAM JAMES LAMPTON (1859–1917),
JUNE WEDDINGS

We find rest in those we
love, and we provide a resting
place in ourselves for those
who love us.

SAINT BERNARD OF CLAIRVAUX (1090–1153)

Two souls with but a
single thought,
Two hearts that beat as one.

MARIA LOVELL (1803–1877),
INGOMAR THE BARBARIAN
(TRANSLATION OF FRIEDRICH KALM)

Grow old along with me!
The best is yet to be.

ROBERT BROWNING (1812–1889),
RABBI BEN EZRA

Keep love in your heart. A life without it is like a sunless garden when the flowers are dead.

OSCAR WILDE (1854–1900)

Love is moral even without legal marriage, but marriage is immoral without love.

ELLEN KEY (1849–1926),
THE MORALITY OF WOMAN AND OTHER ESSAYS

Marriages

are made in heaven.

PROVERB

Marriage has many pains, but celibacy has no pleasures.

SAMUEL JOHNSON (1709–1784), *RASSELAS*

Come live with me, and be my love,
And we will all the pleasures prove
That hills and valleys, dales and fields,
Or woods or steepy mountain yields.

CHRISTOPHER MARLOWE (1564–1593),
THE PASSIONATE SHEPHERD TO HIS LOVE

Come live with me, and be my love,
And we will some new pleasures prove
Of golden sands, and crystal brooks,
With silken lines, and silver hooks.

JOHN DONNE (1573–1631), *THE BAIT*

Let the husband render unto the wife due benevolence: and likewise also the wife unto the husband.

THE BIBLE, I CORINTHIANS 7:3

The amount of women in London who flirt with their own husbands is perfectly scandalous. It looks so bad. It is simply washing one's clean linen in public.

OSCAR WILDE (1854–1900),
THE IMPORTANCE OF BEING EARNEST

If ever two were one,
then surely we.
If ever man were loved
by wife, then thee;
If ever wife was happy
in a man,
Compare with me, ye
women, if you can.

ANNE BRADSTREET (1612–1672),
TO MY DEAR AND LOVING HUSBAND

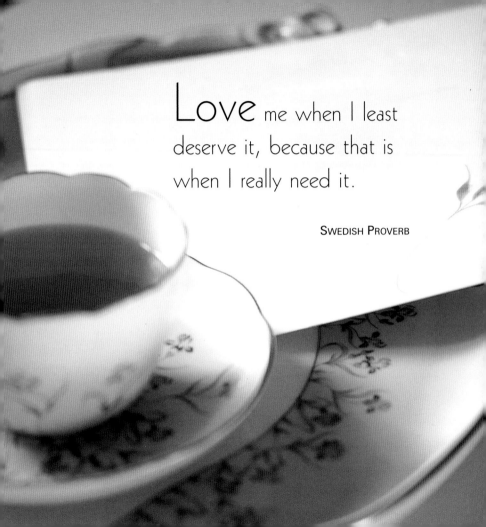

Love me when I least deserve it, because that is when I really need it.

SWEDISH PROVERB

Alma: I rather suspect her of being in love with him.
Martin: Her own husband? Monstrous!
What a selfish woman!

JENNIE JEROME CHURCHILL (1854–1921),
HIS BORROWED PLUMES

Doubt thou the stars are fire;
Doubt that the sun doth move;
Doubt truth to be a liar;
But never doubt I love.

WILLIAM SHAKESPEARE (1564–1616), *HAMLET*

photography credits

Key: a=above, b=below, r=right, l=left

Caroline Arber 4, 61 Jan Baldwin 60b Martin Brigdale 50
David Brittain 2, 6, 14, 41r, 51 Christopher Drake 16
Dan Duchars 47, 54, 55 Melanie Eclare 56a Chris Everard
36r Craig Fordham 1, 62 Catherine Gratwicke 5l, 12 gallery
and bookstore owner Françoise de Nobele's apartment in Paris,
13, 25, 30l, 40, 52 Lulu Guinness' home in London, 63
William Lingwood 34 James Merrell 24, 35 Janie Jackson
Stylist/Designer, 45 Debi Treloar 3, 5r, 10b, 11, 15, 19b,
20a, 21, 28, 29, 32 Annelie Bruijn's home in Amsterdam,
33, 37, 38b & r, 41l, 42, 43, 44, 48, 49, 58, 64
Chris Tubbs 7, 26, 30r Ian Wallace 38a Andrew Wood 8
Paul and Carolyn Morgan's house in Wales, 17, 20b, 22
Polly Wreford endpapers, 9, 10a, 18, 19a, 23, 36l, 46,
53, 56b, 59, 60a Francesca Yorke 27

business credits

Annelie Bruijn: annelie_bruijn@email.com Page 32

Françoise de Nobele Antiquités: 2, rue de Bourbon le
Chateau, 75006 Paris, France Page 12

Lulu Guinness: www.luluguinness.com Page 52

Janie Jackson: Stylist/Designer www.parmalilac.co.uk Page 35